W9-BNN-355

UNDERSTANDING ECONOMICS

TRADE AND EXCHANGE

BARBARA GOTTFRIED HOLLANDER

17:38:30	7.15	870
17:42:05	7.200	4000
17:43:00	7.203	4500
17:43:20	7.20	200
17:43:20	7.190	200
17:44:05	7.31	5000

Britannica®
Educational Publishing
IN ASSOCIATION WITH
ROSEN
EDUCATIONAL SERVICES

To wonderful Ruthie, who has been trading and exchanging (and sharing) since nursery school.

Published in 2019 by Britannica Educational Publishing (a trademark of Encyclopædia Britannica, Inc.) in association with The Rosen Publishing Group, Inc.
29 East 21st Street, New York, NY 10010

Distributed exclusively by Rosen Publishing.
To see additional Britannica Educational Publishing titles, go to rosenpublishing.com.

First Edition

Britannica Educational Publishing
J.E. Luebering: Executive Director, Core Editorial
Andrea R. Field: Managing Editor, Compton's by Britannica

Rosen Publishing
Heather Moore Niver: Editor
Nelson Sá: Art Director
Brian Garvey: Series Designer
Tahara Anderson: Book Layout
Cindy Reiman: Photography Manager
Heather Moore Niver: Photo Researcher

Library of Congress Cataloging-in-Publication Data

Names: Hollander, Barbara Gottfried, 1970– author.
Title: Trade and exchange / Barbara Gottfried Hollander.
Description: New York : Britannica Educational Publishing, in Association with Rosen Educational Services, 2019 | Series: Understanding economics | Audience: Grades 5–8. | Includes bibliographical references and index.
Identifiers: LCCN 2017054427| ISBN 9781538302767 (library bound : alk. paper) | ISBN 9781538302774 (pbk. : alk. paper)
Subjects: LCSH: Commerce—Juvenile literature. | Foreign exchange—Juvenile literature.
Classification: LCC HF353 .H65 2018 | DDC 381—dc23
LC record available at https://lccn.loc.gov/2017054427

Manufactured in the United States of America

CONTENTS

INTRODUCTION

People are always trading things they have for other things they want but do not have. At lunch, you might trade your tuna sandwich for your friend's chicken salad. That seems like a fair exchange for both of you! Trade and exchange depend on both parties getting something they want in a way they feel is fair.

Trade and exchange has gone on for thousands of years. When early humans started to live in cities, they traded things with one another. They also traded items from their cities for things people in other cities had. This is called long-distance trade. For example, people in the eastern Mediterranean region had a special kind of wood called cedar. They would trade it with people in China who had spices and silk.

People living on farms can trade their fruits, vegetables, cattle, and other produce for goods and services available in cities. A farmer might exchange a basket of apples he grew for a pair of shoes someone in town made. This works well for both parties, as long as they agree on the value of the traded items.

Trading today looks different. Many exchanges take place online. Some people make trades on their phones using apps. For example, in 2016, App Ventures Limited updated its Trade n Play app that locates nearby gamers, allows for browsing of their game libraries, and provides a forum for trading video games. Today's trading can also

Trade comes in all forms, like exchanging snacks in school. For a trade to happen, both parties must feel they are benefiting from the exchange.

involve various forms of money from metal coins to currencies based on computer algorithms.

Trade and exchange remain popular in schools. Students trade snacks, school supplies, and fun things like fidget cubes and spinners. Students can trade not just goods but also services—or even goods for services. If you give me a ride to dance rehearsal, I will wash your car or buy you a couple of gallons of gas. When people trade, they offer something in exchange for something else that they need or want.

Money, also called currency, often makes trade and exchange easier. Money provides a way to express the value of traded items. It also acts as an intermediary in the exchange. People use money to engage in trade domestically—in their own countries. They also use money to obtain goods and services from other countries. Having access only to what you can produce is limiting. But through trade and exchange, you can gain access to goods and services produced by others around the world.

CHAPTER ONE

BARTER IT

Bartering is the direct exchange of one good or service for another good or service. Thousands of years ago, people in Mesopotamia (in modern-day Iraq) discovered the benefits of bartering. They traded goods they had for ones they wanted. Many other groups of people did the same thing in the ancient world. Bartering was done in Europe in the Middle Ages. A shoemaker and a farmer might trade their products with each other so that the shoemaker had food and the farmer had shoes. With the use of large ships, people had a way to reach markets in faraway lands. They would take their goods for exchange and bring back goods from those places to their own lands.

People usually bartered goods they had in surplus, or more than they needed. Suppose a person in the Middle Ages wanted to trade his extra fruits for someone else's spices.

Trading goods and services online allows bartering between people living nearby—or far away. Online searches can identify safe sites for online bartering.

To make this exchange happen, the fruit owner needs someone willing to trade spices for fruit. Then, the traders must agree upon a price. How many fruits equal a handful of spices? If the traders traveled great distances by horse to a central marketplace, timing was key. The spice trader would not trade his goods for spoiled fruits!

Today, people also barter online. Some online bartering sites allow trades for personal care services, clothing, home and office space, and transportation. For example, in 2017, Home Exchange operated in more than 150 countries, allowing its members to "trade" homes for vacation stays. SwapStyle members trade clothes, shoes, make-up, and accessories. And BabysitterExchange is a co-op that allows community members to trade services like babysitting and tutoring.

PROS OF BARTERING

In a barter exchange, traders, or parties, seek to gain from an exchange. A trader may be willing to trade a good that she produced too much of for other goods. Or a party may value another person's good more than her own and be willing to exchange. Either way, bartering is a way for people to obtain goods they need or want. When people from different countries or regions barter, they gain access to

A person may own a good, like a jacket, that she no longer values as much as when she first bought it. Trading is a way to exchange these goods for others.

goods they might not have locally. Bartering can expand the pool of available goods.

People also barter services, such as tutoring, housesitting, and babysitting. With services, people are not exchanging physical items. Instead, they are trading their time and effort. Traders may offer services based on what they are good at. For example, a repairman may offer to fix a store's air conditioning in exchange for store credit. Today, some companies engage in bartering called corporate trade. A media company might provide free tickets to a show in exchange for free hotel rooms. Six Flags once bartered free passes to its amusement parks with Orion Trading in exchange for free TV advertisements.

During economic downturns, like recessions, people have less income to spend. Bartering allows people to obtain goods and services without using income. It can also reduce personal expenses. Suppose a house painter is short of cash

Businesses sometimes exchange goods and services with other businesses. Amusement parks might barter entry tickets for free advertisement.

and wants to get a haircut. She knows a hairdresser who wants his house painted. The painter could do some work for the hairdresser in exchange for haircuts. Or let's say a new online advertising and branding agency needs an accountant. It can provide a logo and help design a website for a young accountant in exchange for free accounting services. This kind of bartering happens a lot in today's economy.

Bartering Today

The International Reciprocal Trade Association (IRTA) is a global trade association with more than 100 barter exchanges, corporate trade companies, and complementary currency organizations. A barter exchange consists of two parties that agree by contract to trade property or services. Corporate trade involves trade credits that companies use to obtain goods and services from one another. Complementary currency is a different kind of currency than a country's official currency. It can be used to obtain goods and services. According to the IRTA, bartering generated about $12 billion from more than 400,000 companies worldwide in 2011.

CONS OF BARTERING

Bartering has its advantages, but there are also challenges to this kind of trade and exchange. First, a trader needs someone willing to do the trade. This is sometimes called "double coincidence of wants." Two people have to want to trade for something each wants at the same time. Suppose a person wants to trade her yogurt for an apple. This potential trader needs to find someone who has an apple and is willing to trade it for yogurt. Second, traders must agree on a price in terms of the goods. If one trader thinks one yogurt is worth one apple and the other trader thinks that one yogurt is worth three apples, then the trade might not happen.

Trade and exchange depends on people offering goods that others want. Perishable items, like yogurt, may be traded for others, like apples.

A trade works best if both parties trust each other to provide the goods in the agreed-upon condition at the set price. Bartering with strangers can be risky. On the Internet, for example, a trader might misrepresent a used item as new. When bartering, some people trade only with people they already know and trust, like family and friends. Another problem is that many goods cannot be divided. Two traders may agree that one horse is worth four furs. But if the fur trader has only two furs to exchange, the horse trader cannot divide his horse, and the trade would not happen.

Bartering also involves challenges when it comes to storing goods you want to trade. For one thing, the value of what you have to trade might decrease over time. Fresh apples are worth more the week they are picked than they are a month later. Some goods, like animals, are also expensive to store over time. And if bartering involves a future trade, people must agree about the terms of trade, or common measure of value, both in the present and the future. Currency, such as the American dollar, sets the value at a stable amount and can be used for future purchases. But goods and services may decrease a lot in value over time.

Some goods are easy to store, like clothes or canned goods. Other goods, like animals, involve a lot more care, supplies, time, and money.

CHAPTER TWO

HERE COMES MONEY

Bartering has many advantages. It's a good way to acquire something you want by getting rid of something you don't want as much. But bartering also has disadvantages. In modern society, with millions of people and hundreds of thousands of goods and services, the barter system can be overwhelming. It would be impossible to keep track of how much everything was worth in relation to other things. That's why we use money, or currency. With currency, everyone knows how much a given amount, or denomination, is worth. The dollar in your pocket is worth the same amount at the grocery store as it is at the clothing store.

Currency is what a society or country agrees is the common, acceptable form of exchange for purchasing goods and services. Throughout history, different items from shells to animal teeth to coins have been used as currency. Today, each country has its own form of currency. Exchange rates allow for conversions between currencies of different countries for international trade and exchange.

FUNCTIONS OF MONEY

Money has three main functions. First, it serves as an indirect medium of exchange. Buyers exchange money for goods and services, and sellers accept money to make the sales. Rather than a direct exchange of goods and services like with barter, money is indirect. A person who sells a car does not get a direct good in exchange.

Paper currency is easy to transport. The Bureau of Engraving and Printing, part of the US Department of the Treasury, prints billions of dollars each year.

She gets the indirect good—money—that she can then use to trade for other goods of her choice.

Second, money is a recognizable unit of account. Goods and services have prices, expressed in monetary terms. These terms provide a uniform way to express the items' values and make calculations. Suppose a shirt costs $5 and a pair of pants costs $10. Then three shirts and four

Money is a medium of exchange. People exchange their goods, like cars, for money. Then they can use that money to buy other goods.

pairs of pants costs $55 (without sales tax). In this sale, the buyer trades money in exchange for clothing.

Third, money stores value. It is relatively stable. Many of the items used in bartering were perishable, like cattle and fruit. They were worth more in the present than in the future, which made it difficult to keep track of the exchange. By storing a certain value that remains the same, money gives buyers and sellers confidence to engage in transactions.

TRADING MADE EASIER

Money makes trade and exchange easier in several ways. When people bartered, they had to transport their goods

Cryptocurrencies

On January 3, 2009, a new kind of currency took the financial markets by storm. Bitcoins are not made of paper or metal. In fact, this cryptocurrency is made of bits and bytes and kept in digital wallets. A cryptocurrency is not controlled by a central banking authority (as are individual country currencies). In 2017, other cryptocurrencies included Litecoin, Ethereum, Ripple, Zcash, and Dash.

Consumers use different forms of money to buy goods and services. Cryptocurrencies allow consumers to trade and exchange some goods and services through electronic transactions. Currencies can also be viewed as investments; some investors buy

Bitcoins (BTC) are a cryptocurrency. They use peer-to-peer technology for exchanges. Bitcoins are also open source. Everyone can exchange them throughout the world.

(continued on the next page)

17

(continued from the previous page)

and sell them in hopes of earning more money. They view cryptocurrencies as assets that will gain value over time—sometimes even big gains. For example, although the value of Bitcoins relative to physical currencies fluctuated wildly in the years after its introduction, it eventually rose sharply. An amount of Bitcoins purchased for $100 in 2010 was worth almost $73 million in 2017.

and services to buyers. Transporting heavy items long distances could be a barrier to exchange. But money, like paper currency and coins, is easily transportable in your pocket.

Today's money is also durable. It does not quickly deteriorate. Coins are made from metals, such as gold, copper, silver, and nickel. Paper money is made from strong, thick paper. The average lifespan is about 30 years for a coin and about 15 years for a $100 bill. Both kinds of money change hands many times—that's a lot of trade and exchange!

Money is also divisible. You can break it into smaller amounts to make purchases. For example, a $20 bill can be broken down into two $10 bills or four $5 bills. People can also use a $20 bill for a $15 purchase and receive $5 back in change. With different denominations, or amounts, of paper money and coins, it's easier to figure out how to divide the money you have for the item you want to purchase.

Money is divisible. This $20 can be divided in several ways, such as two $10 bills, four $5 bills, or one $10 and two $5 bills.

Money has value that allows both buyers and sellers to exchange it for goods and services. Suppose someone is selling a cell phone for $500. A buyer can purchase this cell phone in exchange for $500. The buyer knows that the $500 has a value that can be used to purchase any good or service with a $500 price tag.

HELP FROM BANKS

With money came the creation of banks. Banks are institutions that deal in money and its substitutes. From the money that people deposit, a bank makes loans to individuals, businesses, and other banks. There are many kinds of banks that operate within a country's system of trade and exchange.

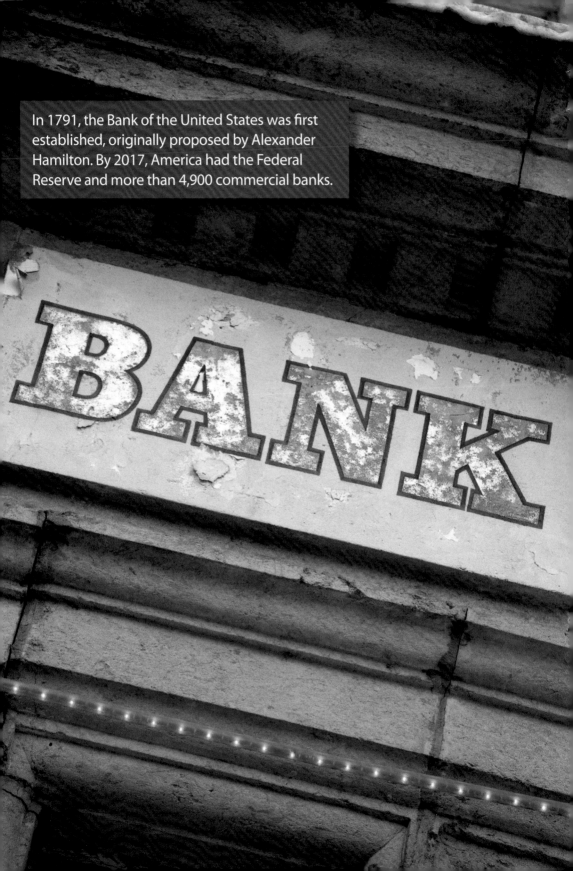

In 1791, the Bank of the United States was first established, originally proposed by Alexander Hamilton. By 2017, America had the Federal Reserve and more than 4,900 commercial banks.

The Federal Reserve, the United States' central bank, sets monetary policy and is responsible for decreasing or increasing the money supply. Decreasing the money supply may decrease economic exchanges since there will be less money available for consumption and investment. Increasing the money supply will likely increase the amount of trade and exchange, because both consumers and investors will have more money to use in the economy.

Banks and other financial institutions facilitate trade and exchange for individuals and businesses. They provide tools, such as checking and savings accounts, that allow people to store money until they are ready to use it to make purchases. They also provide loans that allow people to buy goods and services in the present and repay the purchasing price (with a cost of borrowing called interest) over time.

CHAPTER THREE

MAKING TRADE POSSIBLE

A market is a way for buyers and sellers of certain goods and services to conduct trade and exchange. For example, a car market brings together car sellers and car buyers to offer and purchase cars. A housing market includes people wanting to purchase homes and those involved in selling them.

In a marketplace, sellers present their products by providing a physical display and a price. Suppose a person in the jewelry market wants to sell a necklace. The seller provides potential buyers with a picture, description, or sample of the necklace. The seller also provides a price (or price range) required for purchase.

TRADING PLATFORMS

Businesses have goods and services to sell. How do they find buyers? Buyers have money and want to make purchases.

Selling goods, like jewelry, online can be profitable. Sellers provide a photo of their product and present it with a description and price.

Where can they find sellers? Having the desire and the financial means to trade and exchange are two parts of the process. The buyers and sellers also need a place to come together—either a physical place or an online one.

"Brick and mortar" refers to traditional physical stores, like grocery stores and local clothing businesses. They bring people face-to-face in order to trade and exchange money for goods and services. These stores provide consumers with instant gratification—because they can walk out of the store with their purchases.

Credit and debit cards can be used to pay for online purchases. Online shoppers can find many kinds of goods and services provided by various sellers at different prices.

In 2016, a *Fortune* article reported that "consumers are now doing most of their shopping online." The article cited an estimate that 190 million US consumers were expected to shop online that year. An increasing number of consumers were also using smartphones to make online purchases.

Companies such as Amazon have e-commerce platforms to facilitate trade and exchange. These platforms are software applications that provide online sellers with the means to manage their business operations, like conducting sales. The online marketplace known as eBay brings together people from all over the world. On eBay, sellers can offer all kinds of items, ranging from toys to cars. They provide two buying options—auctioning with bids, or a fixed price. With the auction, the seller sets an opening price and the highest bid (within a specified number of days) wins. With the fixed price option, the first buyer willing and able to pay the price gets the item.

PAYMENT OPTIONS

Credit cards are a very common way for people to make purchases today. In the 1900s, some department stores and oil companies in the United States offered the first versions of store cards for people to use when making purchases at their businesses. The first universal credit card, which could be used at a variety of establishments, was introduced by the Diners Club, Inc., in 1950. Full payment was due at the end of each month. Another major card of this type, known as a travel and entertainment card, was established by the American Express Company in 1958. Under this system, the credit card company charges its

When you use a credit card to pay for a purchase, the seller receives the payment and you owe the credit card company.

cardholders an annual fee and bills them on a periodic basis—usually monthly.

By the late 1950s, major banks introduced cards with something called revolving credit. Cardholders could now use the value in their cards in exchange for goods and services and pay for their purchases later. But rather than repay the amount owed every month, cardholders could carry their monthly balances forward (for a fee). Being able to spend money that can be repaid over a longer period than a month increases the amount of trade and exchange between buyers and sellers.

Debit cards are somewhat similar to credit cards, but they are linked directly to checking accounts, allowing for economic transactions like deducting money to pay for purchases. Prepaid cards are like gift cards. They come with funds preloaded to exchange for goods and services.

Today, many places accept online payment services, such as PayPal. People link their debit or credit cards to their PayPal accounts, which they can then use to instantly transfer funds. PayPal also offers eCheck that is similar to writing checks from a checking account. Easy, convenient, and accepted payment methods increase the likelihood of trade and exchanges.

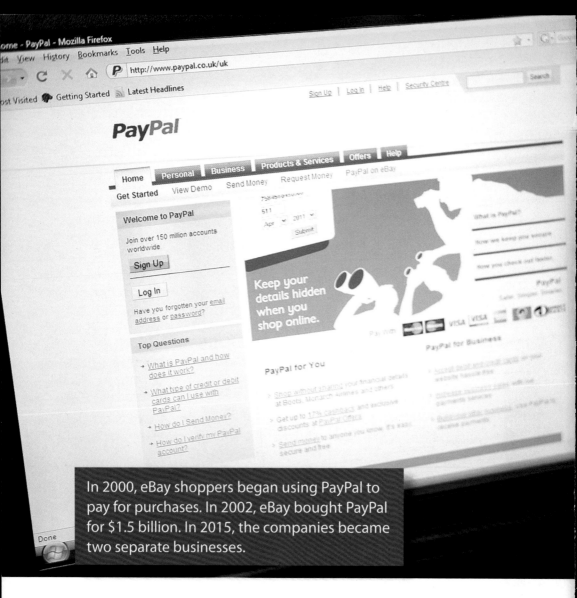

In 2000, eBay shoppers began using PayPal to pay for purchases. In 2002, eBay bought PayPal for $1.5 billion. In 2015, the companies became two separate businesses.

TRANSPORTATION ROUTES

Trade and exchange often involve travel. Hundreds of years ago, people used horses to carry goods. Today, sellers can mail goods to buyers using different carriers, such as UPS, FedEx, or the United States Postal Service. Online purchases often provide shipping options with different

Trade Routes that Changed the World

For centuries, traders have sought routes to transport goods to buyers. The Silk Road, beginning in China and extending to the Mediterranean Sea, is probably the best-known trade route. People used the Silk Road to trade and exchange silk, wool, silver, gold, spices, salt, sugar, fur, metals, gems, and ivory. More than 2,000 years ago, the Silk Road was already increasing trade between different empires.

Other trade routes, both on land and by sea, encouraged trading between Europe and Asia. The Spice Routes brought spices like cloves, cinnamon, and nutmeg from the East to the West. The Incense Route brought goods like frankincense and myrrh from present day Yemen and Oman to the Mediterranean, where it was sold to Roman, Greek, and Egyptian buyers. The Amber Road linked the Baltic Sea and Europe, allowing for the trade of amber beads. Trading tea was also done via the Tea Route, which extended from China to India. Tibetans traded warhorses in exchange for pounds of tea.

delivery dates—the fastest services usually have the highest shipping costs.

Producers of goods use trucks, planes, or ships to transport those goods directly to buyers. They also deliver their products to stores that will then sell directly to consumers.

Online purchases often entail shipping. In 2016, UPS , a leading package delivery company, delivered 4.9 billion packages and documents worldwide.

Producers provide stores with some of their finished goods and keep some as inventory for future sales. For example, a manufacturer of printers may deliver some of its product to stores to sell to consumers and keep the rest of the printers in a warehouse to deliver later.

This process involves a series of exchanges. Manufacturers pay the costs associated with transporting their goods to stores or warehouses. They exchange their money for these services. Store owners exchange their money for the products they buy from the manufacturers. Finally, consumers exchange their money for the products they purchase either from the store or directly from the manufacturer.

CHAPTER FOUR

INTERNATIONAL TRADE

Trade and exchange involves sellers and buyers. With so much trade being conducted internationally today, the supply of goods (from sellers) and the demand for goods (from buyers) has increased a lot. Before looking at international trade, let's consider how supply and demand works.

A seller has a supply of goods and hopes to meet a buyer's demand for his supply. What happens if the demand for the supply is small? For example, you want to sell an old textbook on eBay. As the seller, you set an opening price of $75 and allow potential buyers to bid for the book. After several days, you receive a bid from only one buyer—for $75. The demand is small, and you will have to settle for what the buyer wants to pay. Now suppose that you set the same opening price, but you have 15 people bidding for the book. After several days, the highest bid is $125. More buyers caused an increase in demand that allowed you to receive $50 more than your asking price.

Mobile apps allow shoppers to trade goods and services conveniently, no matter where in the world they live.

Next, consider what would happen if you were a buyer looking for a textbook on eBay. Let's say there is only one seller for the textbook, and many people want to buy it. That means the demand is high, and the supply is low. You will have to pay at least the seller's asking price to obtain the book. In other words, limited supply and high demand benefits the seller. But what if there are many sellers of the same textbook, and you are the only buyer? With an increase in supply, you can now choose between different sellers who are competing for your business. As the buyer, you benefit from this increased supply. You have more options for how much money to spend—and maybe even for the quality of the good (either used or new textbooks).

TRADING PAYS

When people in different countries trade, they expand the supply and demand for their goods and services on a global level. They often trade products for which they possess a comparative advantage. This kind of advantage refers to the ability to produce certain goods and services more efficiently than others. Suppose there is a factory located in the United States and another one located in China. Both factories have the choice to produce clothing, telecommunications, or both.

After much analysis, suppose the American factory appears more efficient at producing telecommunications

Technology has made trading and exchanging worldwide even easier. Buyers choose from products made in different countries, and sellers offer their goods to bigger markets.

equipment than the Chinese factory. The Chinese factory is relatively more efficient at producing clothing. This means that the American factory has a comparative advantage in the production of telecommunications equipment, while the Chinese factory has a comparative advantage in clothing production. Therefore, both countries would benefit if the American company only produced telecommunications equipment and traded with China, and the Chinese company only produced clothing and traded with the United States.

When countries engage in trade, they generally use money. Different countries have different currencies, such as the American dollar, the Japanese yen, the Chinese yuan,

Trading goods and services made in different countries involves exchanging the currency of one country for that of another.

the European euro, and the British pound. Exchange rates allow for currency conversions, or a way to express the value of one currency in relation to another. This allows American buyers to purchase goods from foreign countries using American dollars.

BALANCE IT

International trade involves imports and exports. An import is a good or service that one country buys, or takes in, from another country. Buying imports increases the amount of goods and services available to domestic consumers. Americans can buy American-made cars; but imports also allow Americans to purchase Japanese, German, and Swedish cars in the United States. Imports may offer consumers options at lower prices or options that are unavailable domestically.

An export is a good or service that one country sells to another country. Expanding a seller's market allows for more trade and exchange because the number of potential buyers increases. As with bartering, companies may choose to sell their surpluses of goods or services. Or, a company may be able to sell its goods and services for a higher price in other countries. The profits earned from these sales can be reinvested to increase supply and trade to buyers.

The balance of payments (BOPs) is a way of measuring a country's international economic transactions in a specific time period, like one year. This measurement includes the current account, which documents the value of imports and exports. A current account surplus means that the value of a country's exports is greater than its imports. A current account deficit indicates that the value of the country's imports is greater than its exports. If a country has a current account deficit, that means it owes money to other countries.

Changes in exchange rates affect the value and demand for imports and exports. For example, suppose 1 US dollar can

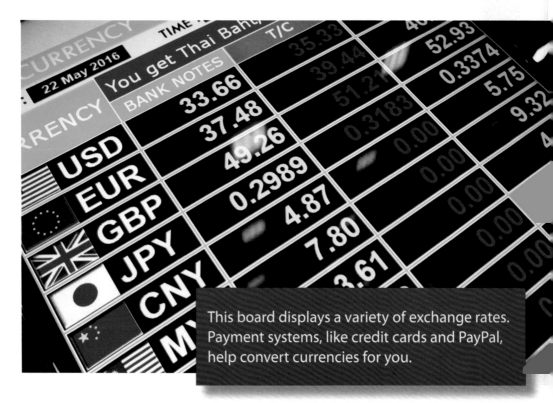

This board displays a variety of exchange rates. Payment systems, like credit cards and PayPal, help convert currencies for you.

Consumer Boycott as Part of the Anti-Apartheid Movement

Countries may use trade restrictions, like quotas and tariffs, to improve their trade balance. Other times, restrictions, like boycotts, are used for political reasons. Boycotts involve voluntarily abstaining from the use or purchase of a good as an act of protest. In 1959, a group in Britain that later became the Anti-Apartheid Movement (AAM) began by calling for a boycott of South African goods such as fruit and cigarettes.

At that time, an all-white government in South Africa was enforcing apartheid—policies of racial segregation and other discrimination. Non-white South Africans were forced to live separately from whites. They could not use the same public bathrooms or marry white people. South African law designated 80 percent of land in the country for the white minority. Non-whites had to carry special documents just to be in these areas.

It took years for South African apartheid to end. In the mid-1980s, many countries imposed economic sanctions on South African exports. Trade between the United States and South Africa was restricted by the

(continued on the next page)

(continued from the previous page)

US Comprehensive Anti-Apartheid Act of 1986, which banned investments and loans to South Africa and prohibited certain South African imports. South Africa finally repealed its apartheid laws in the early 1990s.

be exchanged for .90 euros. An American buyer pays $18 for an imported good from Germany that costs 20 euros. If the exchange rate changed such that 1 U.S. dollar can be converted into .50 euros, that same good now costs $10 for the American buyer. This exchange rate change made the European good relatively less expensive, which can both increase the number of buyers and affect the value of imports.

RESTRICT IT OR TRADE IT

When a country's imports are greater than its exports, it might seek to restrict trade with tools, like quotas or tariffs. Both tariffs and quotas can decrease trade and exchange. A quota, imposed by the government, restricts the number (or monetary amount) of goods or services traded internationally.

A tariff is a tax on an imported good or service, which increases its price. Suppose a buyer can choose between an American-made shirt that costs $7 and a comparable

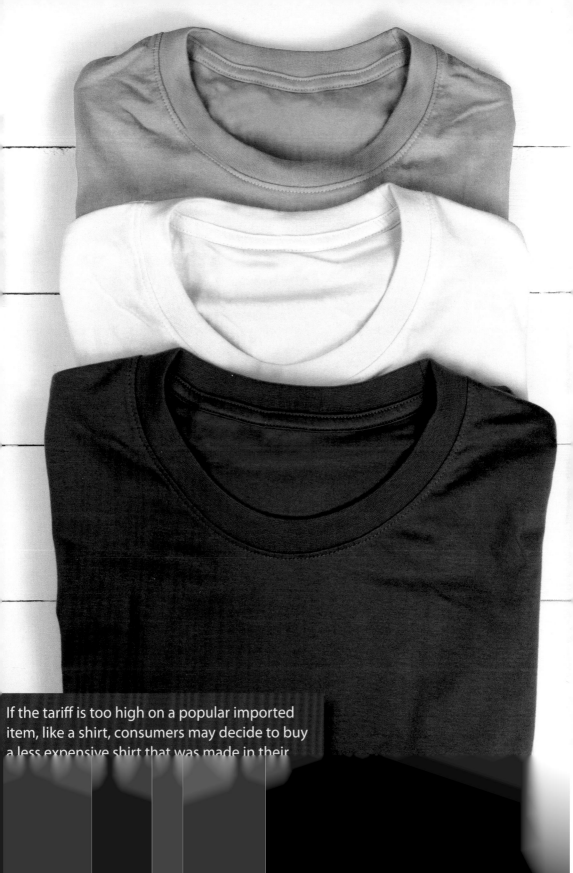

If the tariff is too high on a popular imported item, like a shirt, consumers may decide to buy a less expensive shirt that was made in their

imported shirt for $5. The buyer will most likely choose the less expensive shirt. But if a tariff increases the price of the imported shirt to $8, the buyer may now opt to buy the American-made shirt.

By contrast, trade agreements between countries often seek to promote trade. Countries sometimes make bilateral agreements. That means one country makes an agreement with one other country. Sometimes many countries make a trade agreement. That is called a multilateral agreement. For example, the United States and Canada have a bilateral free trade agreement. But the United States, Canada, and Mexico also formed a multilateral North American Free Trade Agreement (NAFTA) that took effect in 1994. They did this to further increase trade among their nations by seeking to eliminate most tariffs and other restrictions. Just as people look to make the fairest trade for the things they need and want, governments look for the fairest terms of trade and exchange for their country's citizens.

GLOSSARY

BARTER To trade one thing for another without the use of money.

BOYCOTT To join with others in refusing to deal with a person, organization, or country, usually to express disapproval or to force acceptance of terms.

CONSUMER A person who buys and uses up goods.

CREDIT CARD A card one can use to buy things on credit.

CRYPTOCURRENCY Digital currency with computer algorithms that control its supply.

CURRENCY Money in circulation.

DEBIT CARD A card like a credit card used to withdraw money from the holder's bank account immediately at the time of a transaction (as a purchase).

EXCHANGE A giving or taking of one thing in return for another.

EXPORT Good that one country sells to another country.

GOOD Consumable item that is used to satisfy a want or need.

IMPORT Good that one country buys from another country.

INCOME A gain usually measured in money that comes from labor, business, or property.

MARKET A meeting together of people to buy and sell.

MEDIUM OF EXCHANGE Something commonly accepted in exchange for goods and services and recognized as representing a standard of value.

MONEY SUPPLY The total amount of money available in an economy for spending as calculated by any of various methods.

QUOTA A limit on the amount of something that can be traded or imported.

REVOLVING CREDIT Credit renewed as money owed is paid off.

SURPLUS The amount is more than what is required or necessary.

TARIFF Taxes placed by a government on imported items or sometimes exported goods.

TERMS OF TRADE The ratio between the prices of two parties participating in trade.

TRADE The business of buying and selling items; or, an exchange of property without the use of money.

UNIT OF ACCOUNT A monetary unit of measure of value (as a coin) in terms of which accounts are kept and values stated.

VALUE A fair return in goods, services, or money for something exchanged.

Bernstein, William J. *A Splendid Exchange: How Trade Shaped the World*. New York, NY: Atlantic Monthly Press, 2008.

Brennan, Linda Crotta. *Bartering* (Simple Economics). North Mankato, MN: The Child's World, 2012.

Capela, John J. *Import/Export Kit for Dummies*. Hoboken, NJ: John Wiley & Sons, Inc., 2012.

Ceceri, Kathy. *The Silk Road: Explore the World's Most Famous Trade Route with 20 Projects* (Build It Yourself). White River Junction, VT: Nomad Press, 2011.

Furgang, Kathy. *Everything Money: A Wealth of Facts, Photos, and Fun!* Washington, DC. National Geographic Kids, 2013.

Gottfried Hollander, Barbara. *Bitcoins: Navigating Open-Source Currency* (Digital and Information Literacy). New York, NY: Rosen Publishing, 2015.

Herweck Rice, Dona. *Buy It! History of Money* (TIME FOR KIDS® Nonfiction Readers). Huntington Beach, CA: Teacher Created Materials, 2012.

Jenkins, Martin. *The History of Money: From Bartering to Banking*. Somerville, MA: Candlewick Press, 2014.

Parker, Phillip. *The Great Trade Routes: A History of Cargoes and Commerce Over Land and Sea*. New York, NY: Conway, 2012.

Poon, Jessie and David L. Rigby. *International Trade: The Basics*. New York, NY: Routledge, 2017.

Rivoli, Pietra. *The Travels of a T-Shirt in the Global Economy: An Economist Examines the Markets, Power, and Politics of World Trade.* Hoboken, NJ: John Wiley & Sons, Inc., 2014.

Solomon, Michael R. *Consumer Behavior: Buying, Having, and Being.* Boston, MA: Pearson, 2014.

WEBSITES

Ducksters
http://www.ducksters.com/money/stock_markets.php
Facebook: @Ducksters
Twitter: @DuckstersKids

National Association of Trade Exchanges
http://www.natebarter.com
Twitter, Facebook: @NATEbarter

National Geographic
https://www.nationalgeographic.org/activity/the-trading-game

INDEX